JOE NAMATH'S
SUPER BOWL
GUARANTEE

by Patrick Donnelly

SportsZone

An Imprint of Abdo Publishing
www.abdopublishing.com

Greatest Events in
SPORTS HISTORY

www.abdopublishing.com

Published by Abdo Publishing, a division of ABDO, PO Box 398166, Minneapolis, Minnesota 55439. Copyright © 2015 by Abdo Consulting Group, Inc. International copyrights reserved in all countries. No part of this book may be reproduced in any form without written permission from the publisher. SportsZone™ is a trademark and logo of Abdo Publishing.

Printed in the United States of America, North Mankato, Minnesota
102014
012015

Cover Photo: Vernon Biever/AP Images
Interior Photos: Vernon Biever/AP Images, 1, 31, 32, 35, 38; AP Images, 4, 6, 11, 12, 16, 40; NFL Photos/AP Images, 14, 19, 20, 22, 24, 27, 28, 36; Seth Wenig/AP Images, 43

Editor: Chrös McDougall
Series Designer: Craig Hinton

Library of Congress Control Number: 2014944224

Cataloging-in-Publication Data
Donnelly, Patrick.
 Joe Namath's Super Bowl guarantee / Patrick Donnelly.
   p. cm. -- (Greatest events in sports history)
 ISBN 978-1-62403-595-1 (lib. bdg.)
 Includes bibliographical references and index.
 1. Football--United States--History--Juvenile literature. 2. Football players--United States--Juvenile literature. 3. Super Bowl (3rd : 1969 : Miami, Fla.)--Juvenile literature. I. Title.
 796.332--dc23

                                                        2014944224

CONTENTS

Cleveland Browns running back Jim Brown makes a play in a 1958 game. Many potential owners were interested in getting their own NFL teams at the time.

Building the NFL

L amar Hunt had an idea in the late 1950s. The son of an oil tycoon wanted to bring a professional football team to his hometown of Dallas, Texas. So he went to the National Football League (NFL). He was hardly the only one interested at the time.

The league had been around since 1920. But for years, pro football had been in the background. Major League Baseball (MLB) was the most popular sports league. In football, the college game was king. After all, most of the early NFL teams were limited to small cities in the Midwest. Even boxing, track and field, and horse racing were more popular than the NFL.

Baltimore Colts fullback Alan Ameche scores the winning touchdown in the famous 1958 NFL Championship Game.

That had begun to change, though. By the 1940s, most NFL teams were in big cities. And in the 1950s, TV was becoming a bigger part of US culture. More and more people were buying TVs. They tuned into the black-and-white shows for news and entertainment. In 1958, they began tuning in to pro football, too.

The NFL Championship Game was on December 28. NBC TV decided to broadcast the contest between the Baltimore Colts and New York Giants. It was the first pro football game to be shown nationally. Fans were treated to an exciting game. The Colts finally won 23–17 in overtime. An estimated 45 million fans watched. The game became known as the "Game of the Century."

Pete Rozelle realized the importance of that game. He would become NFL commissioner in 1960. Under Rozelle's leadership, the NFL would set up its first national TV deal. That deal helped set a foundation on which the league would grow.

Many others sensed this potential growth, too. Hunt was one of them. So in the late 1950s, he tried get a new team for Dallas. Then he tried to buy the NFL's Chicago Cardinals. Each time the NFL said no. The 12-team league was an exclusive club. Its owners wanted to keep it that way.

Hunt wasn't satisfied with that answer. So he led a group of eight owners in starting a new pro league. The American Football League (AFL) began play in 1960. Its teams were spread across the country. Two AFL teams even played in cities that already had an NFL team. The other six teams were in new markets.

BUMPS IN THE AFL ROAD

Even the NFL initially welcomed the AFL. That quickly changed. Before the AFL played its first game, the NFL tried to hurt the new league. The NFL finally decided to expand. So in 1960, it added the Dallas Cowboys. They would compete directly with Hunt's AFL Dallas Texans. Meanwhile, the NFL also invited the Minnesota Vikings to join in 1961. The Vikings had been planning to join the AFL in 1960. But faced with the opportunity to join the established NFL, they took it. The AFL continued, though. It scrambled to replace the Vikings. The Oakland Raiders were founded and ready for the 1960 season. Then, in 1963, the Texans moved to Kansas City and became the Chiefs. They no longer had to play in the shadow of the Cowboys.

Most people believed Hunt and the other AFL owners were crazy. The NFL was well established. Its popularity was about to take off. This upstart league appeared to have no chance of surviving.

Yet slowly but surely, the AFL grew. The new league had introduced major pro football to new cities. It also appealed to many fans. The AFL positioned itself as the "rebel" league. Owners didn't mind how the players looked. So some players grew their hair long or had bushy beards and mustaches. These characteristics helped make the league more popular with young fans. The fans saw themselves in the league's bold, flashy players. In comparison, the NFL seemed stuffy and old.

What worried the NFL most, however, was money. The AFL offered competitive salaries. So the league immediately attracted

IN THE News

Players might have benefited most from the AFL. The AFL and NFL had to bid for players. This resulted in better salaries for players in the 1960s. The merger returned power to the owners. *Ebony* wrote about the last players to benefit from the two-league system.

> *Nineteen sixty-six will go down as the year the war ended. Not the one in Vietnam, but the hassle between the National Football League (NFL) and the American Football League (AFL). . . . The objects of it all were the high priced bonus babies from the nation's college campuses. Unfortunately, at least for future draftees, this year's crop of rookies is the last of the new-rich, play-for-pay boys. Because of the truce in professional football, college stars must now sign with the club that seeks their services or forget about playing in the US . . . The big payday is over.*

Source: "Last Year for the Big Bonus Babies." *Ebony*, November 1, 1966. Print. 120.

college stars whom the NFL wanted. This trend only increased in 1964. The AFL's TV contract was up after that season. NBC outbid ABC for the rights to show AFL games for the next five years. The new deal was worth five times what ABC had paid in 1960.

With the new TV contract, more fans could watch AFL games. More important, the AFL could offer higher salaries to players.

Soon the NFL finally had enough. The AFL wasn't going away. So the two leagues began talks of a merger.

On June 8, 1966, the leagues announced plans to join forces by 1970. And starting after the 1966 season, the league champions would meet for a true championship game. That game later became known as the Super Bowl.

Star players such as Houston Oilers quarterback George Blanda, *left*, helped the AFL become a true alternative to the NFL during the 1960s.

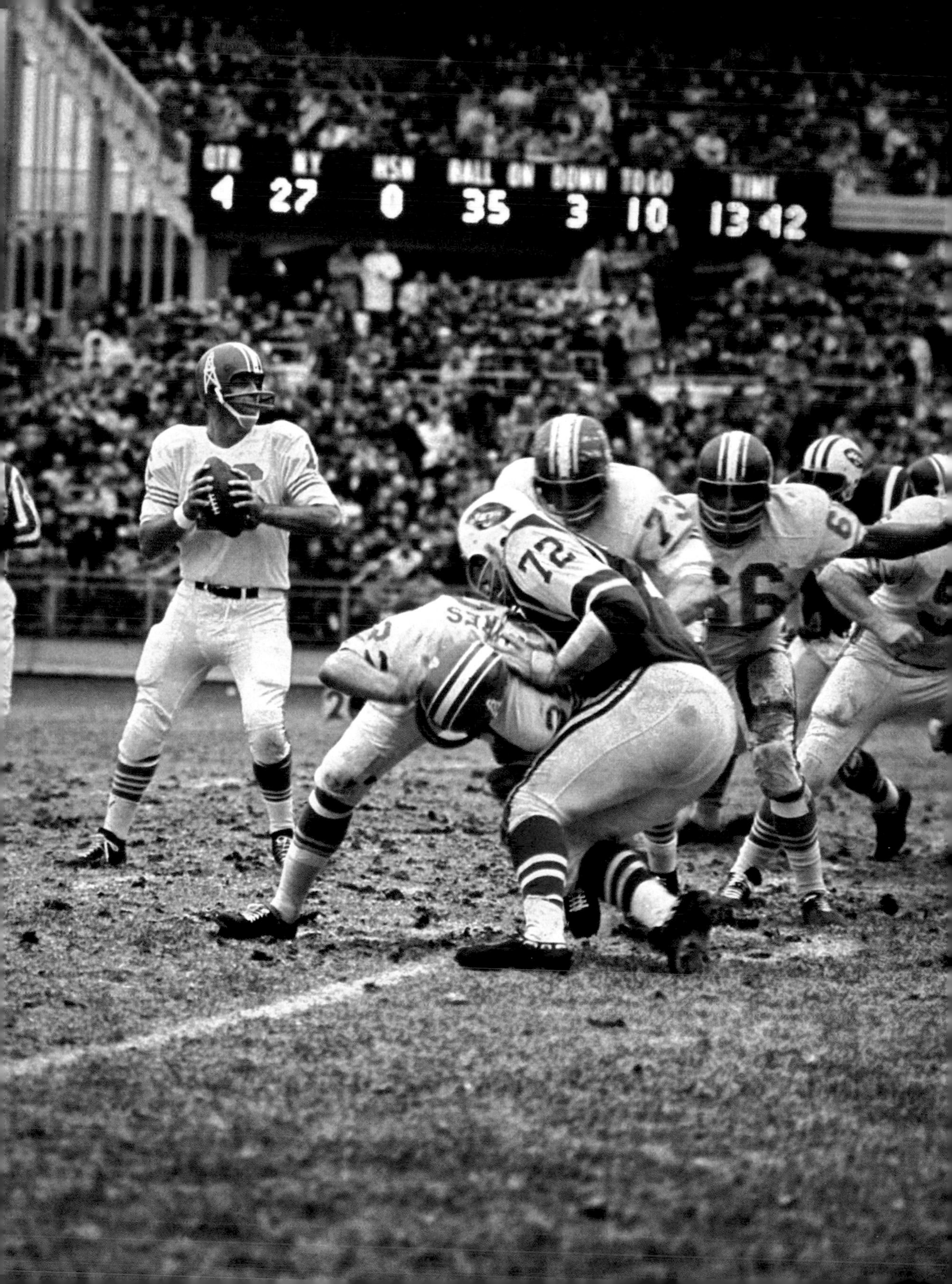
QTR 4
NY 27
0
BALL ON 35
DOWN 3
TO GO 10
TIME 13 42
72
73
66

Joe Namath, *left*, talks with University of Alabama coach Paul "Bear" Bryant during the 1964 college season.

CHAPTER 2

Broadway Joe

The AFL had outbid the NFL for many college players. One of them was Joe Namath. The quarterback had been a star at the University of Alabama. He led the Crimson Tide to a 29–4 record in his three years as a starter. During his senior year in 1964, Alabama went undefeated in the regular season. The Crimson Tide was voted the national champion.

Both NFL and AFL teams wanted Namath. The bidding war began soon after his regular season ended. The St. Louis Cardinals picked Namath twelfth overall in the 1965 NFL Draft. The New York Jets took him first overall in the AFL Draft.

The Jets were desperate for a star player. The team shared New York City with the NFL's Giants. But the Giants were more popular. They had been playing in the NFL since 1925. Jets officials believed Namath could help the team step out of the

Namath gets ready to take a snap during a 1965 AFL game between the Jets and the Oakland Raiders.

Giants' shadow. The Jets also had extra money from the new TV deal in 1964. Meanwhile, playing in New York City intrigued Namath. He had good looks and loads of confidence. If he played well, he could

"THE FOOLISH CLUB"

The NFL was becoming a powerful league in the late 1950s. Few people believed the AFL could challenge the NFL's long-standing dominance. But the eight original AFL owners embraced the challenge. They dubbed themselves "The Foolish Club." And it took them only six years to bring Goliath to his knees. "They started from the back of nowhere. I didn't think they ever would survive," said Gil Brandt, a Dallas Cowboys executive. "They did, and all of the teams are still in operation. They've all done extremely well."

become a star on and off the field in the country's biggest city. So he picked the Jets over the Cardinals.

Namath signed a three-year contract worth more than $425,000. It was the largest contract ever given to a football player. The pressure was on Namath, and he earned every penny.

The Jets had never posted a winning record in their first five AFL seasons. Namath took over as the starting quarterback as a rookie in 1965. They finished 5–8–1 for the third straight year. But success was just around the corner. In 1967, Namath became the first pro quarterback to throw for 4,000 yards in a season. The team went 8–5–1. It was the Jets' first winning record. However, they missed the playoffs by a game. Still, their brash young quarterback had become the brightest star in either league.

Fans were drawn to Namath. On the field he proved to be a confident star. But he was just as popular for his off-field life. He had

Namath poses with a beauty queen after undergoing knee surgery in December 1966.

movie-star looks and lived a playboy lifestyle. Local newspapers loved to write about his social life. Articles covered his favorite nightclubs, his latest girlfriend, and his flashy cars and clothes. Fans nicknamed him "Broadway Joe." It referred to the famous street in New York City.

Namath loved the attention. He enjoyed the nightlife, often staying out until dawn even on the night before a game. He grew his hair long and had thick sideburns. The sports world had never seen anyone like him.

For a less talented player, Namath's lifestyle might have been a distraction. Namath didn't let that happen. He earned the respect of teammates and opponents with his performance. Namath had a rocket arm and steely determination. He became known for leading the Jets to comeback victories. And he was tough. Namath had been suffering from knee trouble since college. As a professional, he dealt with bruises and broken bones. Yet he never missed a game due to injury in his first five pro seasons.

"He was so good, such a competitor, so wonderful for the league," Paul Maguire, a punter and linebacker for the rival Buffalo Bills, said years later. "You know how when Tiger Woods is in a tournament, you turn on the TV, and when he's in contention, you can't look away? Same with Joe. When he came to town, everything stopped. Everyone just wanted to see Joe."

Namath became the face of the AFL. But NFL fans still didn't give the league much respect. In their minds, Namath was the perfect representative of the AFL. They considered it to be a league that favored style over substance. And those people had good

IN THE News

Joe Namath took his job for the Jets seriously. But he enjoyed his time in the spotlight, too. *Sports Illustrated* wrote about his popularity in a 1966 story.

Joe is not pleading to be understood. He is youth, success, the clothes, the car, the penthouse, the big town, the girls, the autographs, and the games on Sundays. He simply is, man. The best we can do is catch a slight glimpse of him as he speeds by us in this life, and hope that he will in some way help prepare us for the day when we elect public officials who wear beanies and have term themes to write.

Source: Dan Jenkins. "The Sweet Life of Swinging Joe." Sports Illustrated, October 17, 1966. Web. Accessed August 25, 2014.

reason to believe that. The AFL and NFL champions had faced off in the first two Super Bowls. Both times the NFL's Green Bay Packers had easily won. There was little reason to doubt that the NFL's streak would continue in 1968. That's when Namath and the Jets put together a season that set pro football on its ear and changed its history forever.

Namath sets up to pass during a 1967 game against the Oakland Raiders.

Namath and the Jets opened the 1968 season with a 3–2 record before taking off.

CHAPTER 3

The Guarantee

T he Jets opened the 1968 season slowly. They won only three of their first five games. The team caught fire after that, though. It won eight of its final nine regular-season games. The only loss came against the Oakland Raiders. But New York got payback against the Raiders in the AFL Championship Game. The Jets were trailing midway through the fourth quarter. Then Namath hit star wide receiver Don Maynard for the go-ahead touchdown pass. The Jets' defense held on for the 27–23 victory.

That win sent the Jets to Super Bowl III two weeks later in Miami, Florida. To most fans, the win also meant that the Jets were doomed. Their opponents would be the Baltimore Colts. The Colts had cruised through the NFL season with relative ease. They went 13–1 on the strength of a stingy defense. Baltimore held opponents to 10 or fewer points 10 times

Baltimore Colts quarterback Earl Morrall, *left*, talks with coach Don Shula, *right*. Most people believed the Colts would easily win Super Bowl III.

that year. The Colts destroyed the Cleveland Browns 34–0 in the NFL Championship Game. And many fans considered that to be the true championship game. The Colts defeating the Jets was viewed as a given.

The oddsmakers agreed. Baltimore was an 18-point favorite to win Super Bowl III. By the time the game rolled around, the line had

THE *HEIDI* GAME

The Jets' 1968 loss to the Oakland Raiders was one of the most famous games in pro football history. The game was November 17 in Oakland, California. New York led 32–29 with slightly more than a minute to play. But the game ran long. NBC was broadcasting the game. The network decided to cut away to show the start of its scheduled Sunday night movie, *Heidi*. It proved to be a huge mistake. The Raiders scored two touchdowns in nine seconds to win 43–32. NBC's phone system was jammed with angry viewers. Because of that fiasco, TV networks no longer cut away from games in progress.

moved to 20 points in some places. The gamblers who set the lines were showing the Jets no respect. The nation's fans followed suit.

That disrespect got under Namath's skin. He knew the Colts were good. But he thought the Jets were better. And he had no problem sharing that opinion with anyone who asked him. He was particularly annoyed with talk of Earl Morrall. The 34-year-old Colts quarterback was the definition of old school. He had a square jaw and a flat-top haircut, and he wore black cleats. And many reporters had suggested that Morrall was the better quarterback in the matchup. They had a point. He had led the NFL in passing while filling in for injured legend Johnny Unitas. Morrall also threw 26 touchdown passes that year compared with Namath's 15.

That didn't matter much to Namath. He watched countless hours of Colts game film to prepare for the Super Bowl. What he

Daryle Lamonica (3) led the Oakland Raiders to Super Bowl II after the 1967 season. However, they lost to the Green Bay Packers.

saw was a quarterback who succeeded by throwing short passes against weak defenses. Namath wasn't afraid to say as much after the AFL Championship Game. He said Oakland Raiders quarterback Daryle Lamonica was a better passer than Morrall. The Jets arrived in Miami a week before the Super Bowl. Reporters were eager to see if Namath would hide from that quote.

"I said it, and I meant it," Namath told them. "Lamonica is better."

The Super Bowl hasn't always been viewed as a super game. The game now known as Super Bowl I was held in January 1967. More than 32,000 seats went unsold. The NFL champion Green Bay Packers dominated. They easily beat the AFL champion Kansas City Chiefs, 35–10. As the *New York Times* reported, few were surprised with the outcome.

The outcome served to settle the curiosity of the customers, who paid from $6 to $12 for tickets, and a television audience estimated at 60 million, regarding the worth of the Chiefs. The final score was an honest one, meaning it correctly reflected what went on during the game. The great interest had led to naming the event the Super Bowl, but the contest was more ordinary than super.... The Super Bowl games will now go on year after year, but it may be some time before an [AFL] team will be good enough to win one, especially if the [NFL] champion comes from Green Bay.

Source: William N. Wallace. "Green Bay Wins Football Title." New York Times, January 15, 1967. Print. 1A.

He wasn't done, though. Namath said three other AFL quarterbacks were better than Morrall, too. These quarterbacks were the San Diego Chargers' John Hadl, the Miami Dolphins' Bob Griese, and Namath himself.

When not practicing, Namath often hung out at the Jets' hotel. Many times, he could be found sitting by the pool. All week, reporters gathered around to ask him questions. And all week, Namath said he thought the Jets were the better team.

The Colts could not believe what they were hearing. Baltimore coach Don Shula said, "I don't see how Namath can rap Earl. He's thrown for a great percentage without using dinky flare passes. . . . Anyone who doesn't give him the credit he deserves is wrong."

The aging Unitas was healthy enough to dress as a backup to Morrall for the Super Bowl. He said Namath wasn't prepared for the Colts' fearsome defense.

"He's never faced anybody like he's going to have to face in our defense," Unitas said. "Our pass rush will be something, I think, that Namath will remember for a long time."

Even other NFL coaches couldn't resist taking shots at the Jets and the AFL. Atlanta Falcons coach Norm Van Brocklin had been an NFL Most Valuable Player (MVP). He said, "On Sunday, Joe Namath will play his first professional football game."

Joe Namath's guarantee brought extra attention to Super Bowl III.

Eventually, Namath had enough. On the Thursday before the game, he attended a banquet honoring him as pro football's player of the year. During his acceptance speech, a Colts fan began heckling Namath. The quarterback decided it was time to spell it out in no uncertain terms.

"The Jets will win on Sunday," Namath said. "I guarantee it."

THIRD WORLD CHAMPIONSHIP GAME / JANUARY 12, 1969, ORANGE BOWL, MIAMI, FLORIDA / PRICE $1.00

CHAPTER **4**

Shocking the World

Jets coach Weeb Ewbank heard about Namath's guarantee. But he didn't think much of it. At least that's what he said publicly.

"I wouldn't give a darn for him if he didn't think he could win," Ewbank told writers.

Baltimore coach Don Shula appreciated the comment. His team was favored by nearly three touchdowns. Shula had worried his players might start to get a bit smug. Namath's guarantee, Shula thought, would keep his team focused on proving the Jets' quarterback wrong.

Attention leading into the game focused on Namath. That gave the impression that Namath was the team's only star.

IN THE News

Namath's guarantee showed the confidence he had in his team. But that confidence clearly wasn't shared by the national media. It was only after the game ended that it began to dawn on the writers and fans that Namath had been right all along.

Whatever slim hopes the Jets had of winning centered on Namath's arm—and the only thing he seemed to be exercising was his mouth. . . . Who were the Jets trying to kid? Didn't they know that the youngsters in the AFL were no match for the tough old pros in the NFL? Hadn't they heard that the rugged Baltimore defense, which held three teams scoreless in regular season play, made a specialty of manhandling uppity quarterbacks?

As it turned out for the Jets, the role of the underdog has its psychological advantages. Besides, Namath's confidence was catching. By the time the Jets took the field they had more going for them than Joe's wide-open passing attack.

Source: "Impossible Reality." Time, January 24, 1969, Vol. 93, Issue 4.

But the Jets had other strengths. New York had a strong running attack that year. Fullback Matt Snell and halfback Emerson Boozer combined to rush for more than 90 yards per game. And the Jets

Namath prepares to take a snap during Super Bowl III.

defense finished second in the AFL in interceptions. The team

would need these unsung heroes to step up to have a chance.

The Jets came into the game well prepared. Coaches and

players studied game film during the week before the Super Bowl.

AFL LIVES ON

The AFL introduced some new ideas to football. Some of those ideas stuck even after the merger. The AFL was the first league to put players' names on the backs of their jerseys. The two-point conversion was a staple of the AFL. The NFL later adopted the play in 1994. The AFL also was the first to put the official game clock on the scoreboard. Before then, only the referee knew how much time remained in a game.

Baltimore had a slow, methodical offense. The Jets found many holes in the Colts defense, too. Namath had sounded crazy when he said publicly that the Jets would win. But behind the scenes, the Jets players began to agree with him. Tight end Pete Lammons even stood up during one team meeting.

"You'd better turn off the film," he said, "because we're going to get overconfident!"

Most fans saw Namath as being overconfident. In his locker room, though, his confidence spread. "For him to guarantee it gave [us] ripples of confidence," Jets cornerback John Dockery said. "OK, he believes it. We believe it, and we can do it."

During the season, Namath and the Jets were known for the long pass. So the Colts came out prepared to stop the play.

Namath prepares to hand the ball off to running back Emerson Boozer in Super Bowl III.

Little did they know, the Jets weren't planning to use it. Speedy Don Maynard was Namath's favorite downfield target. But Maynard was hobbled by a pulled hamstring. He played, but was used mostly as a decoy. Instead, the Jets came out running. Snell chewed up hunks of ground at a time. The Colts had problems handling his combination of size and speed. They stacked the line of scrimmage to try to stop the run. But then Namath picked them apart with short passes to sure-handed receiver George Sauer.

The first quarter was scoreless. But Namath led the Jets on an 80-yard drive in the second. Most of the yardage came on quick passes to Sauer or runs by Snell. The burly fullback finally bowled over two Colts for a four-yard touchdown. That gave the Jets a 7–0 lead.

New York's defense flustered Earl Morrall all day. He had been the NFL's leading passer. Yet Morrall completed just six of 17 passes for 71 yards. He also threw three interceptions. Meanwhile, the Jets offense kept chipping away. They didn't score another touchdown. But Snell ran 30 times for 121 yards. Meanwhile, Namath made smart decisions in a conservative passing attack. Three Jim Turner field goals gave New York a 16–0 lead in the fourth quarter.

Jets running back Matt Snell runs with the ball during the fourth quarter of Super Bowl III.

Unitas was called upon from the bench. The Colts hoped he could recapture his former MVP form. Unitas did finally get the Colts on the scoreboard. But it was too little, too late. The Jets held on to win 16–7.

It wasn't the prettiest game. But it was a win just as Namath had guaranteed. And as the quarterback jogged into the locker room, he held his right index finger high above his head. The Super Bowl MVP wanted to remind people one more time which team—and which league—was number one.

Namath runs off the field after leading the Jets to victory in Super Bowl III.

The Kansas City Chiefs beat the Minnesota Vikings in Super Bowl IV. The win further confirmed that the AFL could compete with the NFL.

CHAPTER 5

Bigger
and Bigger

O ne season remained before the AFL-NFL merger happened. The Jets' Super Bowl win had shown some people that the AFL was a legitimate league. Still, many believed the win had been a fluke. They still believed the NFL was foolish to merge with the weaker AFL. Then the underdog AFL champion won Super Bowl IV. This time, the AFL's Kansas City Chiefs steamrolled the NFL champion Minnesota Vikings 23–7.

In 1970, the AFL was no more. Its 10 teams joined with three NFL teams to create the American Football Conference (AFC). The remaining 13 NFL teams became the National Football Conference (NFC). Today each conference has 16 teams. Their champions still face off in the Super Bowl.

Commissioner Pete Rozelle took over in 1960 and helped the NFL become the United States' most popular sports league. He retired in 1989. In 2014, a Forbes.com article credited Rozelle's foresight for the league's success.

Who knew that Sunday NFL viewing would become not only popular, but part of the American culture? Or that the Super Bowl would turn into a de facto national holiday? Even Rozelle himself couldn't have predicted that his work would carry the league to billions a year. But billions it is. In good times and bad, the NFL remains a license to print money. The Rozelle model is still at work, bigger than ever.

Source: Tom Van Riper. "Pete Rozelle's Legacy Lives On." Forbes.com. Forbes.com, December 15, 2011. Web. Accessed August 8, 2014.

Before Super Bowl III, some NFL fans viewed the game as a novelty. The NFL Championship Game was the true test. That quickly changed. AFC teams won nine of the next 11 Super Bowls. Five of those wins came from former NFL teams. It didn't matter, though. The playing field had been leveled.

Commissioner Pete Rozelle made many changes that helped the NFL grow more popular.

Upon taking over in 1960, commissioner Pete Rozelle had set a foundation for the NFL to grow. At the time, teams operated independently. That meant teams in bigger cities often made more money than those in smaller cities. Rozelle changed that. In 1962, he negotiated the NFL's first national TV deal. The teams would share the money equally. Rozelle also got the teams to share other revenues. These moves helped ensure that all teams were competitive. They also set up the NFL for huge growth. Then Joe Namath came along and kick-started the growth.

Today, the NFL is easily the most popular sports league in the United States. Regular-season and playoff games drew record crowds in 2013. Some 25 million fans play fantasy football. TV ratings continue to break records. Meanwhile, the Super Bowl has become an unofficial national holiday. In February 2014, the broadcast of Super Bowl XLVIII was the most-watched TV show in

The modern Super Bowl has become an unofficial national holiday in the United States.

US history. With 111.5 million viewers, it broke the record set a year earlier by the broadcast of Super Bowl XLVII.

The 1968 season proved to be the peak for Joe Namath and the Jets. Injuries and off-field distractions took their toll on Namath. The Jets, meanwhile, haven't been back to the Super Bowl through 2014. In the history of the big game, though, their legacy lives on.

TIMELINE

1920
The NFL is founded in Canton, Ohio.

1958
An estimated 45 million people watch the NFL Championship Game, the first nationally broadcast NFL game.

1960
The AFL begins play with eight teams spread across the United States.

1961
NFL commissioner Pete Rozelle negotiates the league's first national TV contract.

1965
After being drafted in both the AFL and the NFL, University of Alabama quarterback Joe Namath decides to play for the New York Jets in the AFL.

June 8, 1966
The NFL and AFL announce that they will merge after the 1970 season. Beginning with the 1966 season, the two league champions begin facing off in the Super Bowl.

January 15, 1967
The NFL champion Green Bay Packers easily beat the AFL champion Kansas City Chiefs in Super Bowl I. The Packers again win Super Bowl II in January 1968.

1968
Namath leads the Jets to an 11–3 record in the regular season. The Jets advance to the Super Bowl.

January 9, 1969
On the Thursday before Super Bowl III, Namath famously guarantees that the Jets will beat the heavily favored Baltimore Colts in the game.

January 12, 1969
Namath leads the Jets to a 16–7 victory over the Colts in Super Bowl III.

February 2, 2014
Super Bowl XLVIII becomes the most watched TV event ever in the United States when 111.5 million people tune in.

commissioner

The chief executive of a sports league.

contract

A legal agreement for service between two parties, such as a player and a football team.

decoy

Something designed to distract.

draft

A system used by sports leagues to spread incoming talent among the league. Each team picks a new incoming player, usually in order of worst to best record from the previous season.

flare pass

A short throw, usually to a running back or wide receiver behind the line of scrimmage.

markets

The entire areas surrounding large cities.

merger

When two parties combine into one.

methodical

Done in a systematic or organized way.

novelty

Something unusual.

oddsmakers

People who determine the probability that something will happen so others can bet on whether it will or not.

playboy

A man who lives an extravagant lifestyle.

rookie

A first-year player in a league.

FOR MORE INFORMATION

SELECTED BIBLIOGRAPHY

Felser, Larry. *The Birth of the New NFL: How the 1966 NFL/AFL Merger Transformed Pro Football*. Guilford, CT: Lyons Press, 2008. Print.

Gruver, Ed. *From Baltimore to Broadway: Joe, the Jets, and the Super Bowl III Guarantee*. Chicago, IL: Triumph Books, 2009. Print.

Kriegel, Mark. *Namath: A Biography*. New York: Viking, 2004. Print.

Miller, Jeff. *Going Long: The Wild 10-year Saga of the Renegade American Football League in the Words of Those who Lived It*. Chicago, IL: Contemporary Books, 2003. Print.

Roberts, Randy, and Ed Krzemienski. *Rising Tide: Bear Bryant, Joe Namath, and Dixie's Last Quarter*. New York: Twelve, 2013. Print.

FURTHER READINGS

Howell, Brian. *Football*. Minneapolis, MN: Abdo Publishing Co., 2012. Print.

Robinson, Tom. *New York Jets*. Edina, MN: Abdo Publishing Co., 2011. Print.

Scheff, Matt. *The Best NFL Quarterbacks of All Time*. Minneapolis, MN: Abdo Publishing Co., 2013. Print.

Wilner, Barry. *The Super Bowl*. Minneapolis, MN: Abdo Publishing Co., 2013. Print.

WEBSITES

To learn more about the Greatest Events in Sports History, visit **booklinks.abdopublishing.com**. These links are routinely monitored and updated to provide the most current information available.

PLACES TO VISIT

Green Bay Packers Hall of Fame
1265 Lombardi Ave.
Green Bay, WI 54304
(920) 569-7512
www.packers.com/lambeau-field/hall-of-fame/visit.html
The Green Bay Packers are one of the oldest teams in the NFL, and they were the league's dominant team in the 1960s. The Packers won the first two Super Bowls. The hall of fame, which is located at the Packers' Lambeau Field, has exhibits that highlight the great players and moments in the team's history.

Pro Football Hall of Fame
2121 George Halas Dr. NW
Canton, OH 44708
(330) 456-8207
www.profootballhof.com
This hall of fame and museum highlights the greatest players and moments in the history of the National Football League. A new class is enshrined prior to each season. The celebration includes an NFL exhibition game. The Lamar Hunt Super Bowl Gallery at the Hall of Fame chronicles the history and stars of each Super Bowl through artifacts and interactive exhibits.

INDEX

ABOUT THE AUTHOR

Patrick Donnelly is a veteran sportswriter who has covered the NBA, NFL, MLB, NHL, NASCAR, PGA, and college and prep sports for the Associated Press, MLB.com, and other websites and publications throughout the United States. He lives in Minneapolis, Minnesota, with his wife and two daughters.